General

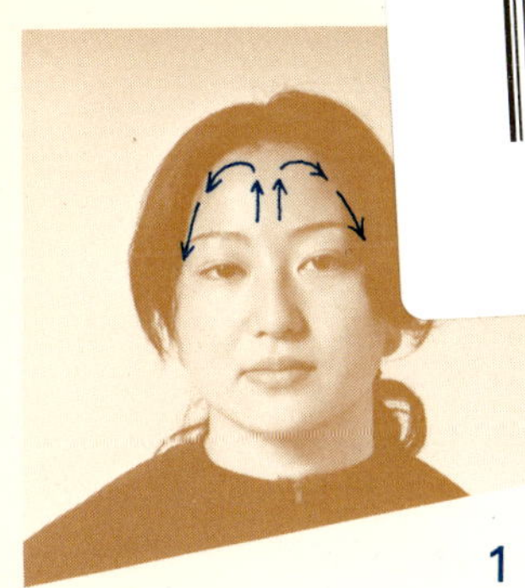

1

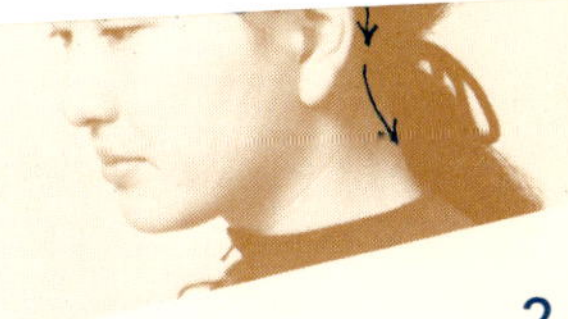

2

3

4

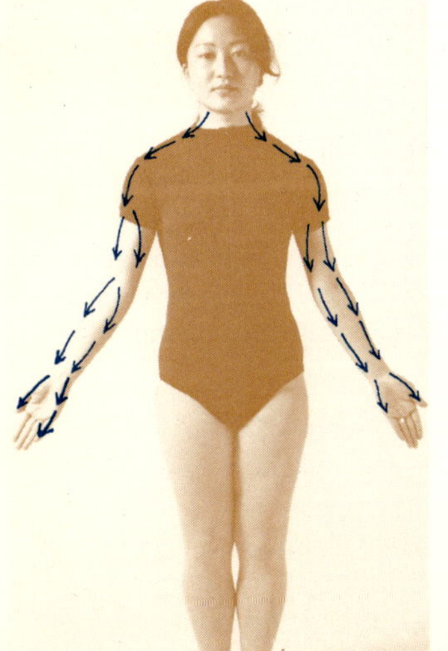

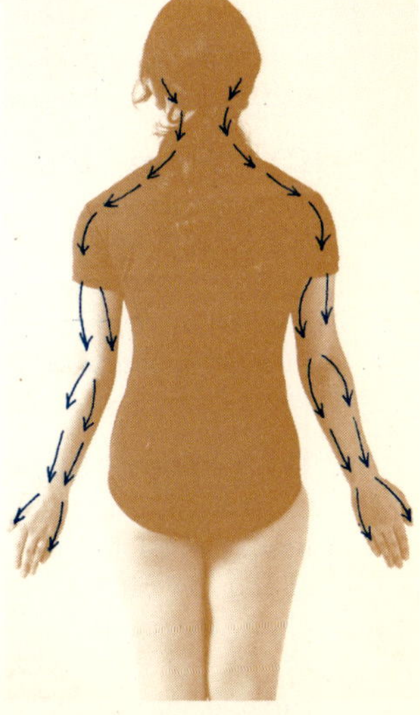

3 BASIC PRINCIPLES OF CHINESE MASSAGE

B) From "Light" to "Heavy"

"TUI-NA" or Chinese Massage is applied in the following manner : the first touch is administered lightly. To judge the patient's sensitivity, gradually the amount of pressure exerted is increased until it is adequately strong for the patient, then the pressure is decreased to the original first or "light" touch. This allows the tissue to recover from the heavy stimulating pressure which has a stagnating effect on the local blood circulation and causes a disagreeable sensation.

C) From "Slow" to "Rapid"

Hurry, speed, great rapidity are to be avoided. There is a natural rhythm in all things and in "TUI-NA."

The rhythm is an essential aspect of the manipulation. The slow, rhythmic movements are to be developed through practice as one would learn the rhythm of a waltz.

D) From "Superficial" to "Deep"

The soft "light" touch mainly effects the superficial tissues while the deeper body structures are reached by strong pressure. In giving the massage in fracture cases, the first application is the "light" one. To locate the area of distress, the pressure can be changed to a suitable one.

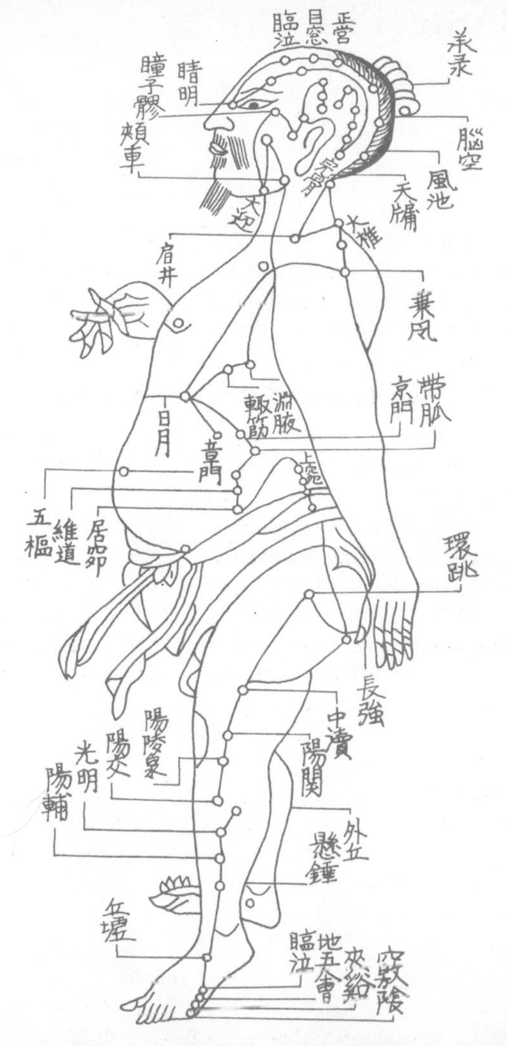

正營
目窗
臨泣
承灵
瞳子髎
睛明
顴髎
頰車
天迎
眉井
腦空
風池
天牖
大椎
秉風
京門
帶脈
輒筋
淵腋
日月
章門
五樞
維道
居髎
上窌
環跳
長強
中瀆
陽關
陽陵泉
陽交
光明
陽輔
外丘
懸鍾
丘墟
臨泣
地五會
俠谿
竅陰

2 BASIC PRINCIPLES OF CHINESE MASSAGE

There are some basic laws to be considered in the application of "Tui-Na" or Chinese Massage that should be understood and applied to obtain optimum effects and to avoid undesirable effects in a given condition treated.

A) Two Types of General Massage

In doing General Massage, it must be done systematically. Haphazard or random treatment will be ineffective and is injurious to the body tissues.

TYPE ONE begins at the point between the eyebrows, then to the forehead, along the hair-line all the way to the neck, then shoulders and down the arms.

TYPE TWO begins as in TYPE ONE at the forehead, but on reaching the neck, the course of massage applications descends the back to the sacrum, then follows the bone crest and on down the leg.

One or both of these procedures can be used in 2 or 3 repetitions. The last moves in General Massage are the stretching by pulling and moving (shake) of the small finger and small toe.

Positions : 1) Sitting
then
2) Lying position
or
3) Side lying

This is "going from a point to a line" and all over the body, and imparts a feeling of general well-being.

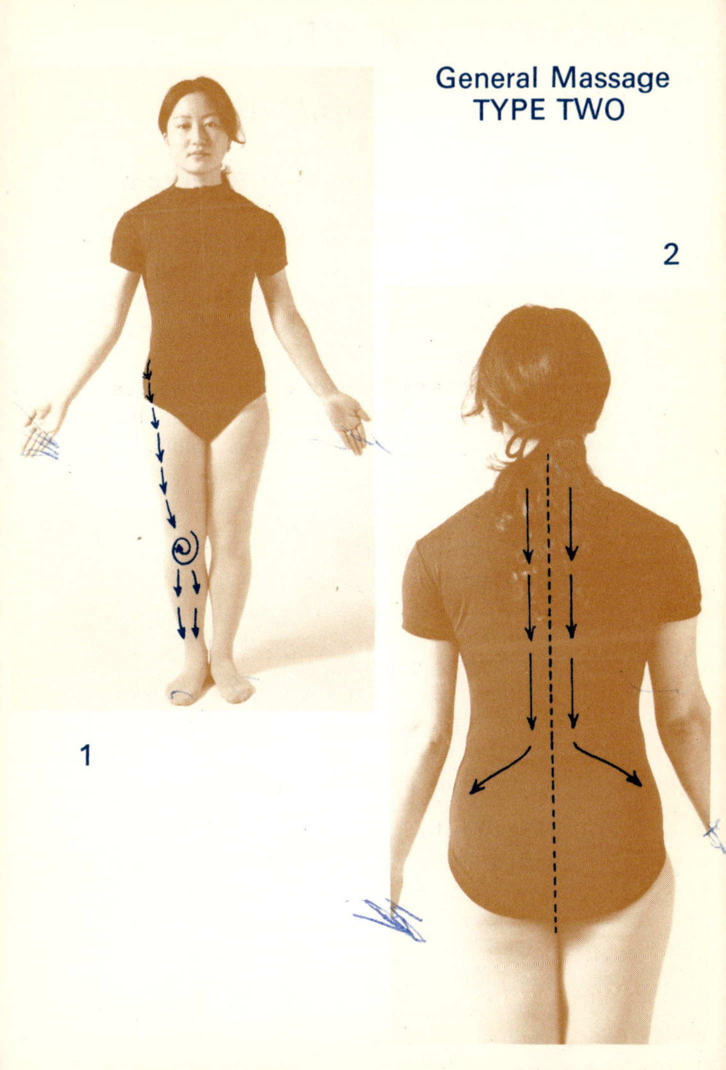

2
1

4 BASIC PRINCIPLES OF CHINESE MASSAGE

E) Order of Treatment of Symptom

Should the complaint be manifest in one area only, the selection of the technique to be applied is simple.

In case of multiple symptoms presenting, the selection of the order of treatment should be based on "urgency" or the most distressing symptom should be attended to first.

In the case of a patient having dizziness, nausea and vomiting, these can be symptoms of fainting, and we should treat to prevent shock. Other symptoms should be attended to later.

F) Selection of the Order of Techniques

When a condition is in the chronic stage, the whole body will require treatment and it is done in the following order :

1) Head to Body
2) Back to Front
3) Trunk to Extremities
4) Upper extremities to Lower extremities
5) Left side to Right side

G) Flexibility

Rigidity is to be avoided. Do not adhere unchangingly to a set pattern, but be flexible towards your patient, for there is great difference from patient to patient, from part to part in the same patient as well as from bow to bow.

The Ancient Chinese Masters stated it clearly. "If your hands and heart know the secret, that is THE LAW and the techniques change."

General Massage

After the manipulation, let the patient stretch
the elbow joints horizontally two or three times.

5 TUI (Pushing) A

Both hands apply pressure on the area treated with a slight back and forward movement, without leaving the point of contact till it causes redness.

With the thumb pad, press and move up and down or sideways.

WHERE APPLIED: Head
Forehead
Neck
Ribs
Children

Note: When Dr. Manaka received TUI-NA in China, the practitioner combined a slight vibratory movement to the TUI-NA technique which was most effective and agreeable.

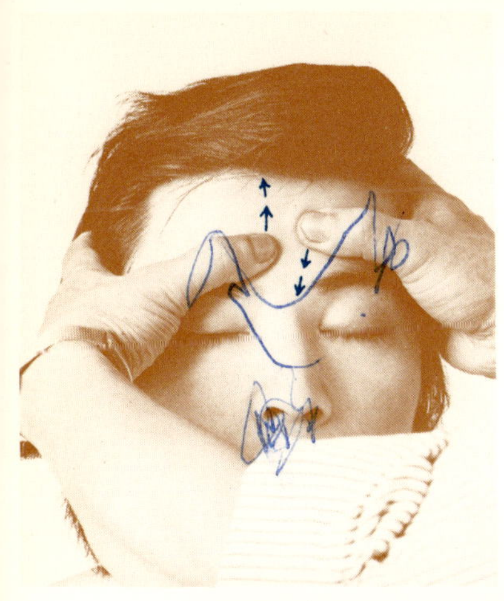

TUI A for forehead

TUI A to ribs

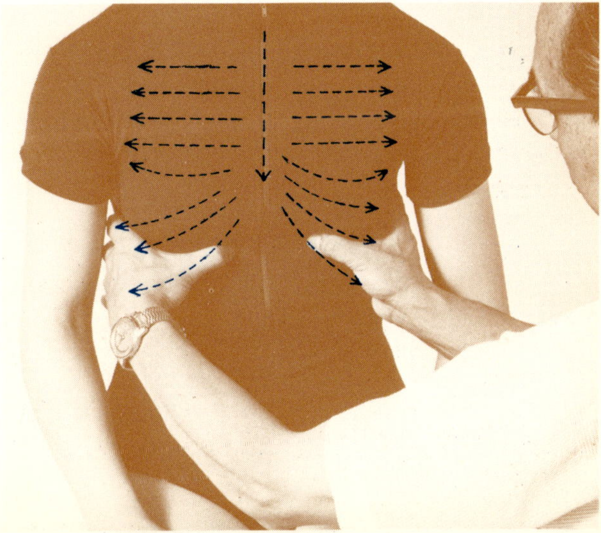

6 TUI (Pushing) B

Make a fist, thumb folded inside, with knuckles being prominent and comb-like.

Hand position is to be as shown in photos, but move it vertically on the body with a rolling motion.

WHERE APPLIED:
Back
Concave aspects of elbow and knee
Thigh
Back of neck

Note: Some lubricant will be added for a feeling of comfort, when this technique is applied lightly.

TUI B to back

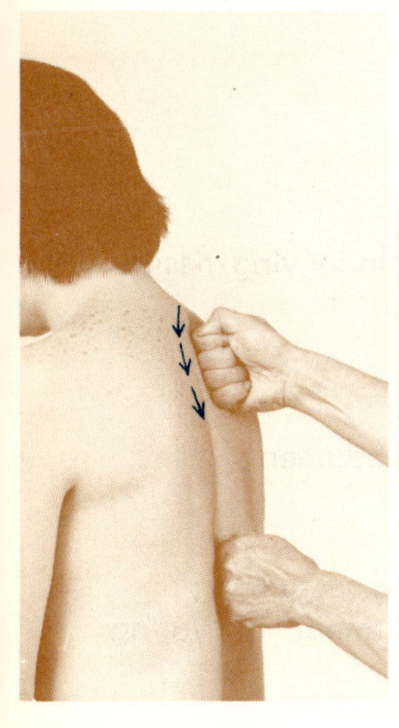

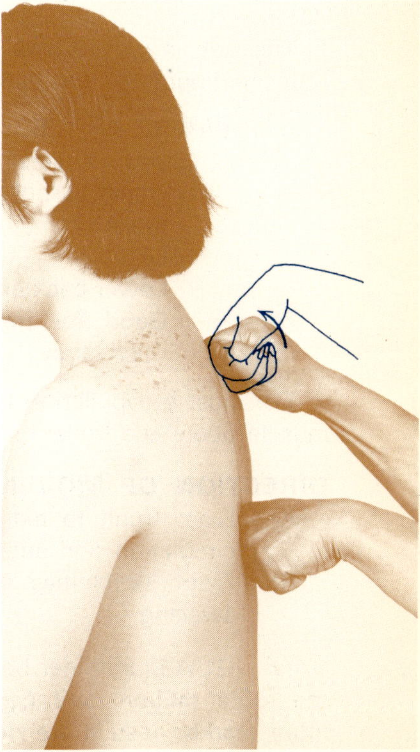

7 TUI (Pushing) C

The skin is moved over underlying tissues with the finger tips and pads.

> WHERE APPLIED:
> (Soft body areas)
>> Upper part of abdomen
>> Waist
>> Legs
>> Lower back and sacrum
>> Good for treatment of young children

TUI must be applied in the direction of the muscle fibers and bones.

DIRECTION OF MOVEMENT:

A) From trunk to extremities: increase circulation and energy.

B) From extremities to trunk: reduce swelling.

Note: GUA in stronger bodied individuals is the same motion, and can be done where more marked results are desired, by using a hard object, such as a coin, glass bead.

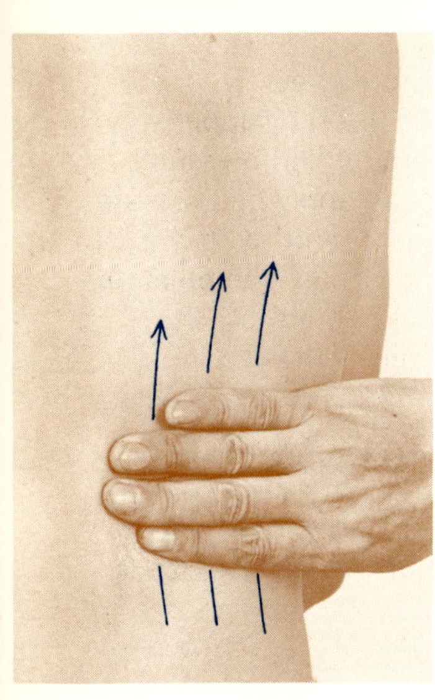

TUI C to back

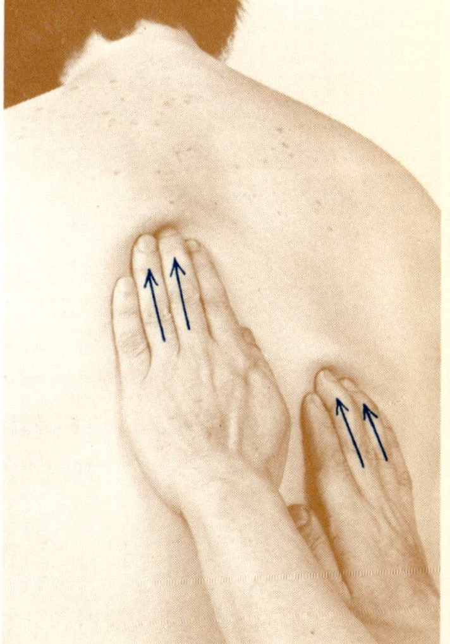

8 TUI (Pushing) D

This has a slight vibratory effect.

TUI movements can be given by application of vibration to one part, while pressure is applied to opposite part, by applying pressure on the forward movement and with much lighter pressure with the same manipulation going backwards on the same areas:

Push forward 3 times, then

push, moving backwards 3 times.

NA (Pinching Forward)

This is a forward pinching movement, by using fingers and palm of the hand to cause redness.

Fingers are against thumb, as shown in photo.

NA is very effective in relief of pain, and reduction of swelling.

WHERE APPLIED: Muscle groups
Tendons

DIRECTION OF MOVEMENT:

From below to upwards (or reverse)

Note: To facilitate the application of TUI, NA, and NING (mentioned at the next page,) the skin may be moistened with hot or cold water, wine, oil, to prevent excessive skin irritation or injury.

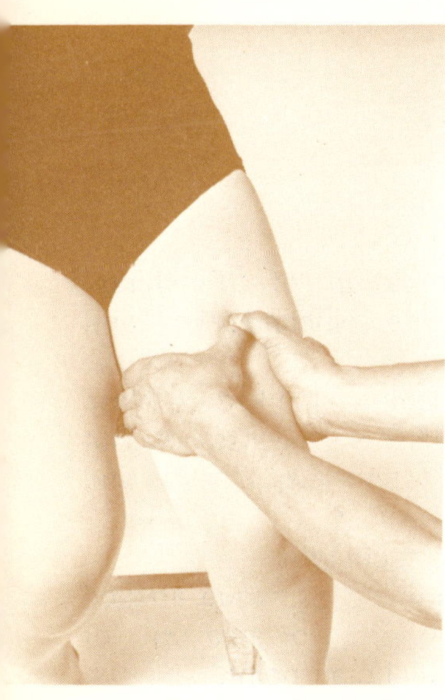

TUI D
to lower extremities

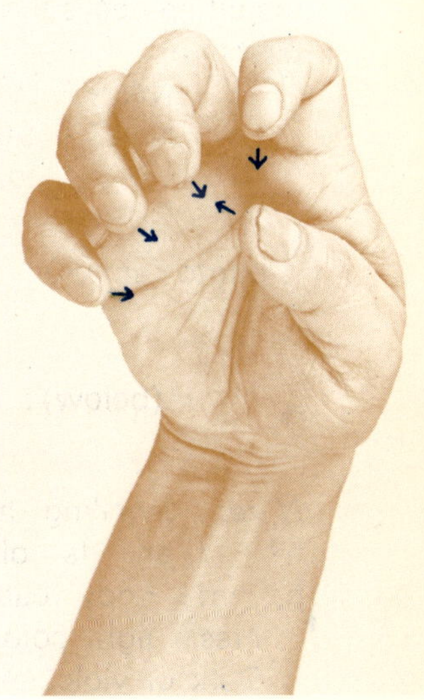

NA

9 NING (Nipping a Point)

NING is an application of "Pinching" followed by lifting the pinched skin and releasing it.

NING is repeated until marked redness appears. Therefore, NING is similar to NA. But the difference is the location of application and direction:

NA = Moving technique

NING = Stationary technique applied to one spot or area only or one meridian point.

photo (above): NING with scissor action of index and middle finger bent.

(below): NING with thumb and other fingers.

Note: Swelling may appear at the point treated, and its color will differ according to patient's body reaction:

Fresh, light color = Coolness, Depletion.

Dark or violet color = Heat, Fullness.

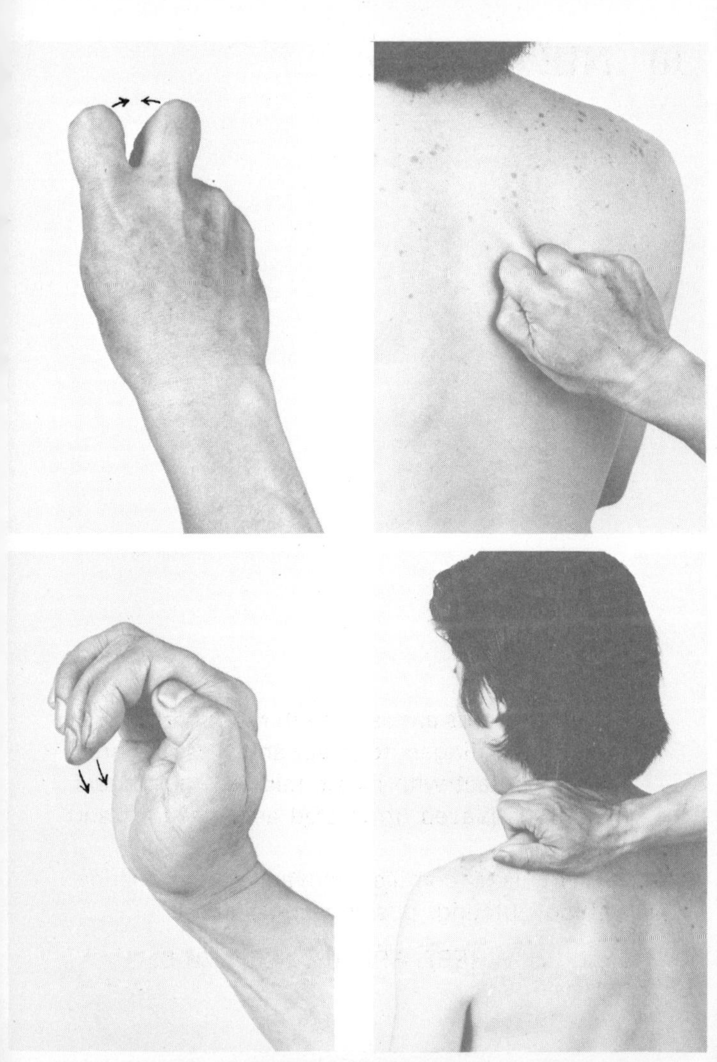

10 NIE (Twisting)

Both hands are used, with thumbs opposing each other fingers together and twist the area. Also, contact with index, middle, ring fingers, thumb is placed on treated area, then lift and rotate.

NIE is a complex movement of twisting, lifting, rotating, pushing and pulling.

WHERE APPLIED: Lower back

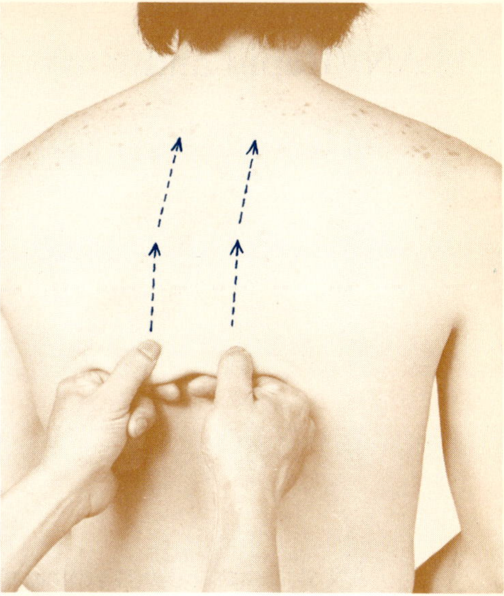

NIE to back

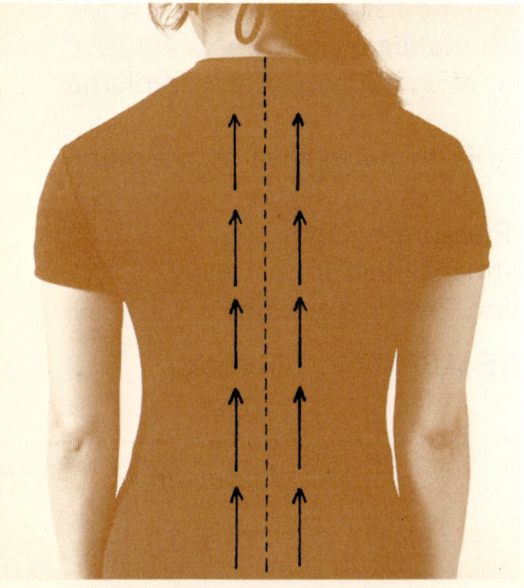

11 AN (Rapid and Rhythmical Pressing)

AN is a rapid and rhythmical pressing with the thumb, palm of hand, back of clenched hand. Often both hands are used.

Palm is most effective, when used on large areas.

The pressure is to be relative to condition treated:

    Starting Pressure = Light
    Mid-Treatment Pressure = Heavy
    Termination Pressure = Light

       WHERE APPLIED: Temples
                             Chest
                             Back
                             Abdomen

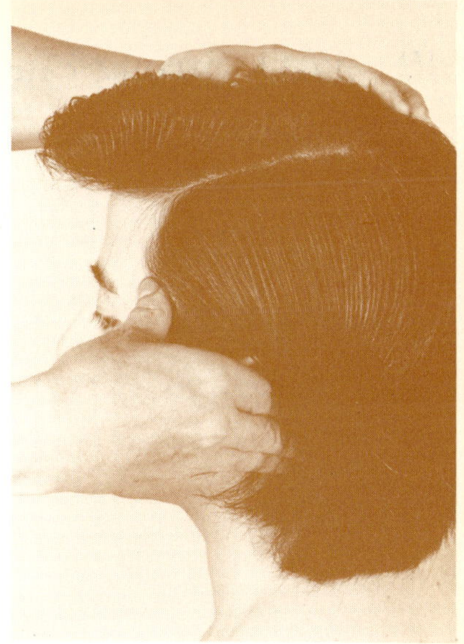

AN to temple

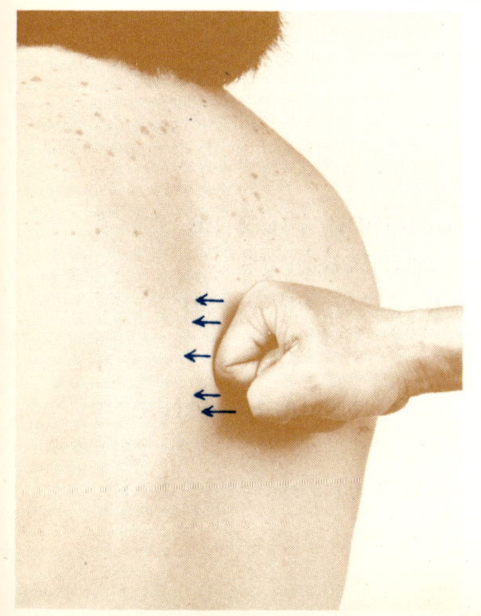

AN to back

12 TAO (Strong Pinching Pressure)

TAO is a strong pinching pressure on a point, done by thumb and forefinger.

TAO is used in an emergency, such as fainting.

Note: There is a striking similarity between these points shown in photos and the "Revival" points of KUATSU as used in Japanese Judo.

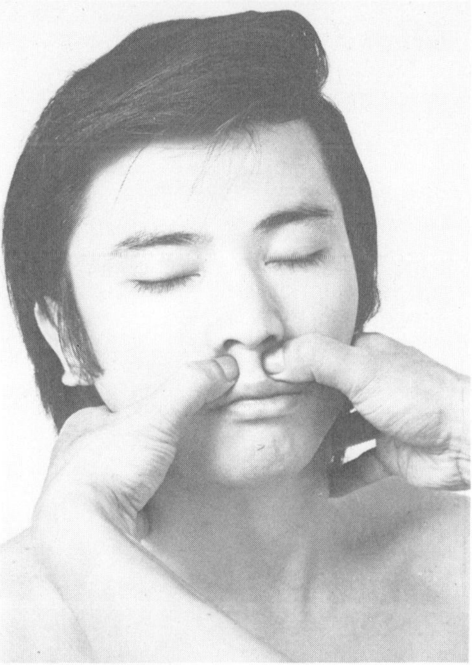

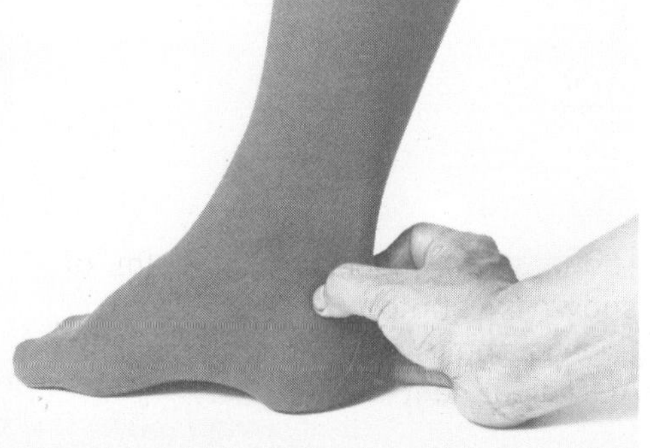

13 MA (Rubbing)

MA is similar to TUI (Pushing,) but lighter, and applied to painful areas and surroundings.

Use palm of hand and thumb or other finger tips.

Both hands may be used by putting palms together and applying small finger side of hand.

Note: In bruising, MA is often used to disperse it.

PAI (Tapping)

PAI is done with finger tips or palm of hand, as shown in photo.

PAI is given strohgly to the back of the knee in LUMBAGO treatment.

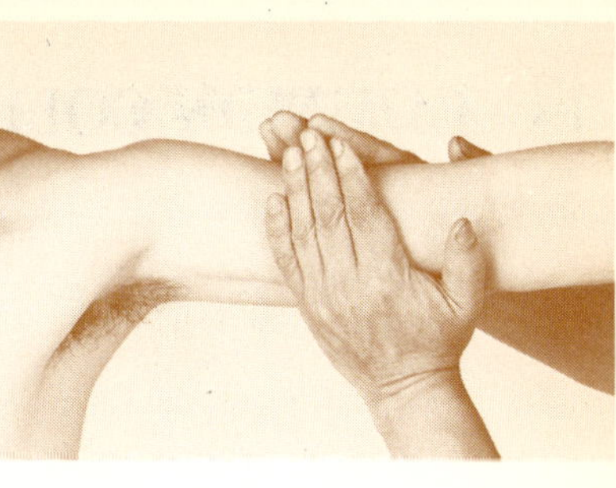
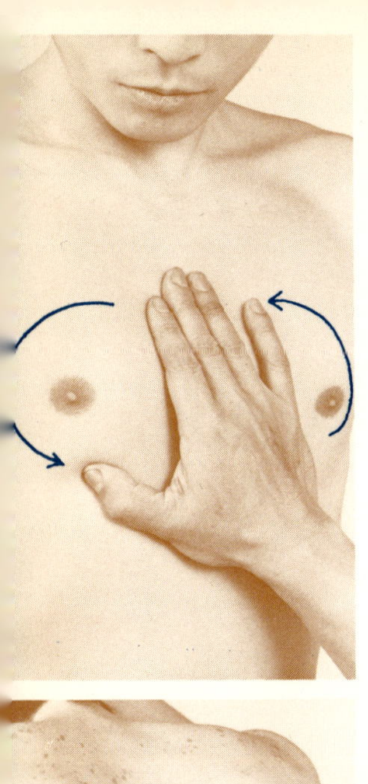
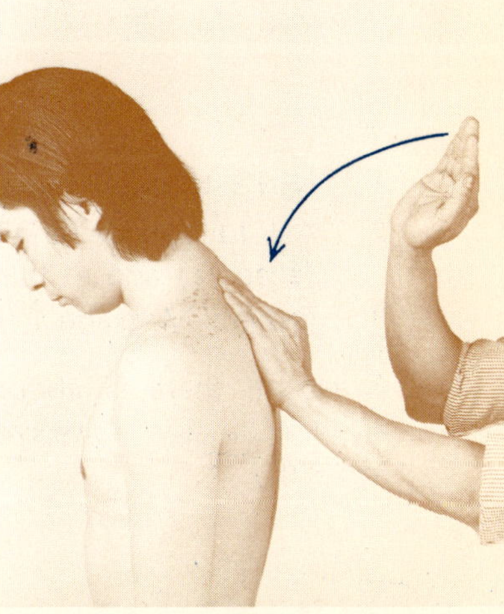
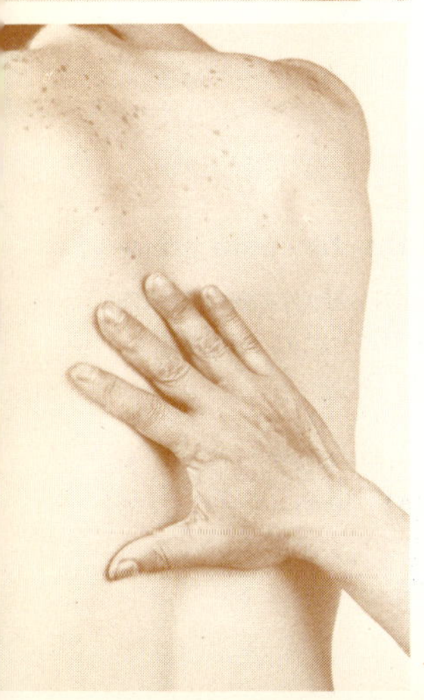

MA

PAI to back

14 COMMON COLD

1. NING to back, along the thoracic spine.
2. AN to outside angle of shoulder blade (scapula) and at third thoracic vertebra.
3. General Massage TYPE ONE.

Note: If there is abdominal upset, MA to abdominal area (clockwise) and TUI C of sacrum.

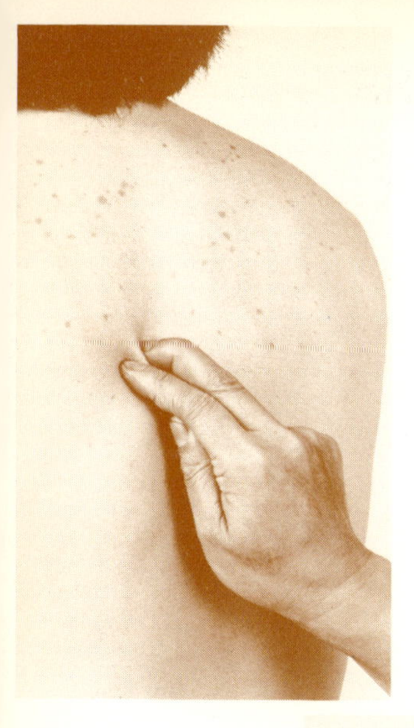
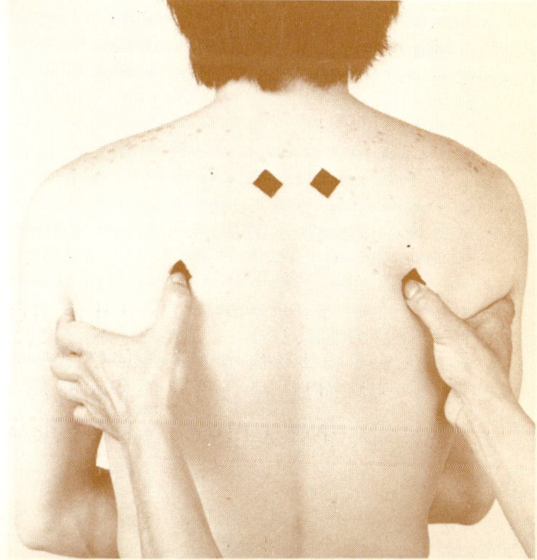
NING to back
AN of scapula

15 SLEEPLESSNESS

Treat 2 or 3 hours before retiring.

1. TUI A between the eyebrows, going up forehead to hair line, 10 to 15 times.
2. General Massage TYPE TWO.
3. TUI C or D to the sole of the feet.
4. NIE to back, from below upwards.

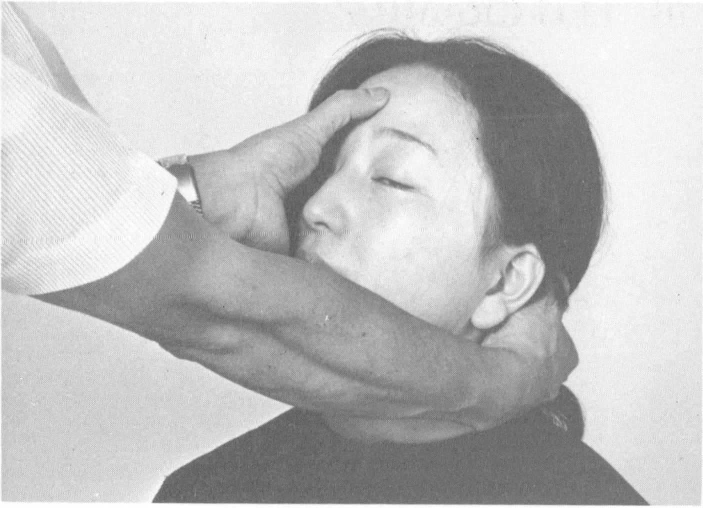

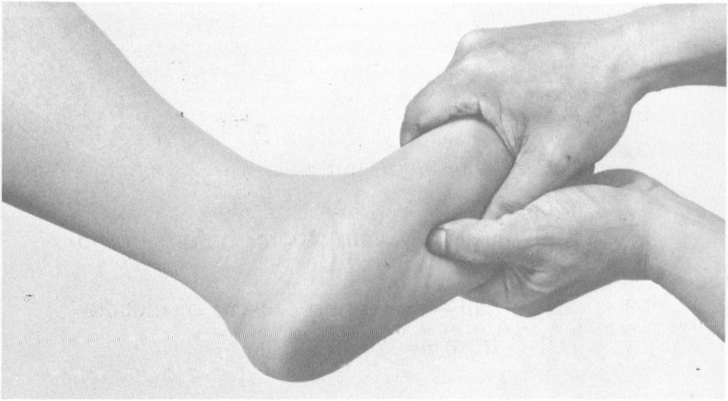

16 LEG CRAMPS

1. NA to lower extremities.
2. NING or PAI to back of knee.
   Rub hands to warm them, before doing this.
3. AN to calf—inside and outside of muscle.
4. TUI C from above to below.

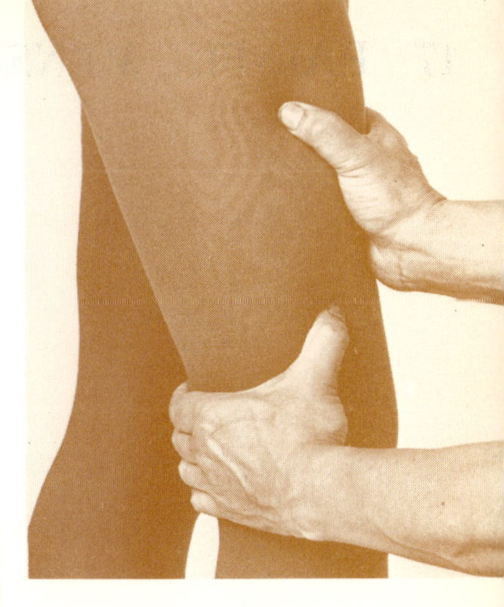

NA to lower extremities

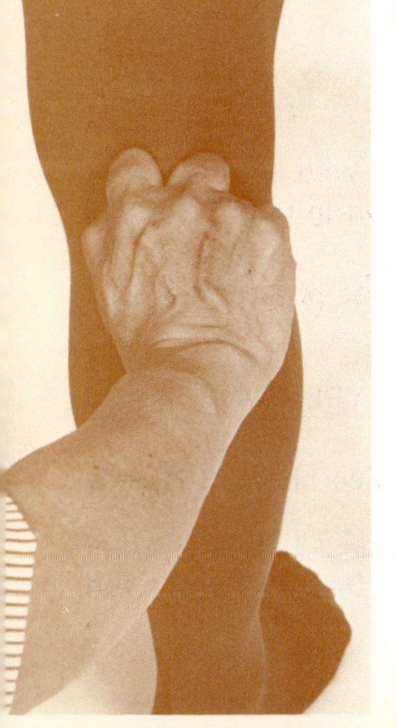

NING to back of knee

17 PAINFUL MENSES

For back pains:
1. AN to point in line with level of navel.
2. AN to points shown in photo (left) at page 22.
3. TUI C to sacrum. See photo (above.)

For low abdominal pains:
1. General Massage TYPE TWO (back to legs.)
2. MA of abdomen. See photo (below.)

PREVENTION: 4 or 5 days before onset of menses, AN with warmed hands to waist and over kidneys.

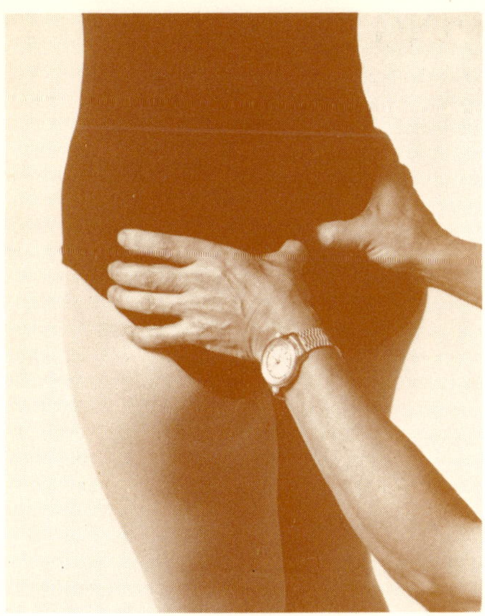

TUI C to sacrum

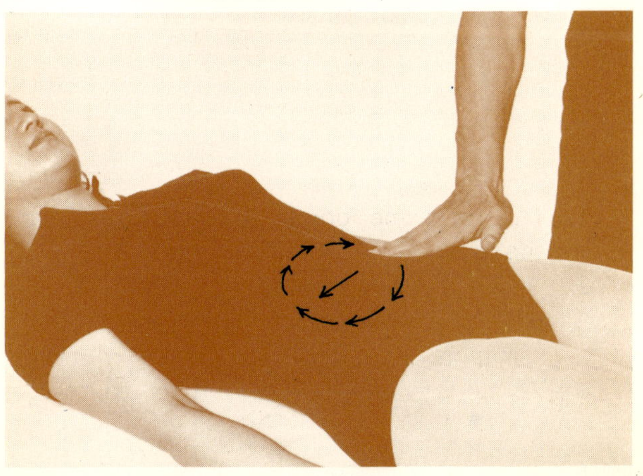

MA of abdomen

18 WHOOPING COUGH

1. AN of same points in photo (left) at page 22.
2. NING to back of neck.
3. General Massage TYPE TWO. Upper position only.
4. TUI A of chest.

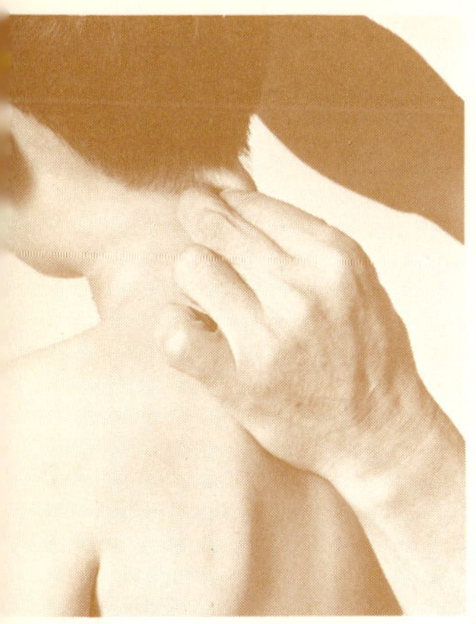

NING to back of neck

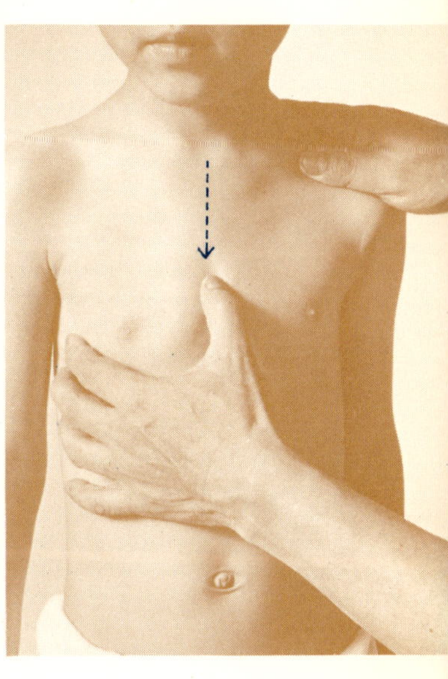

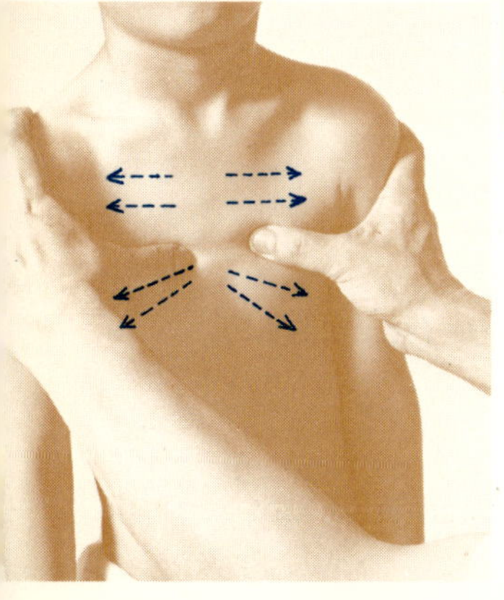

TUI A of chest

19 DIARRHEA

1. TUI C of sacrum.
2. NA of shoulder blade (scapula.)
3. TUI A of waist.
4. MA of abdomen.

For children: AN to center of foot.

NA of scapula

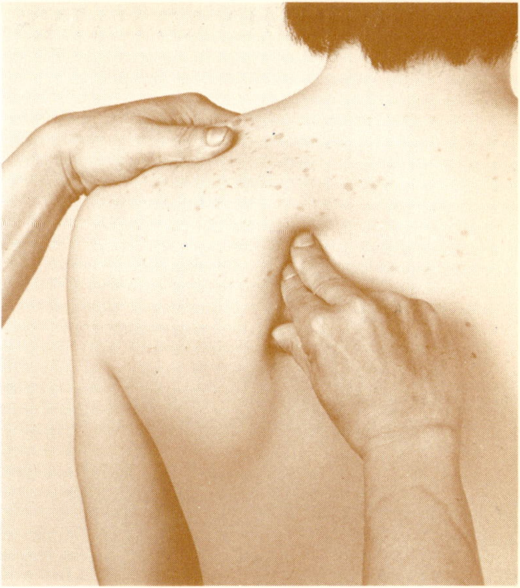

TUI A of waist

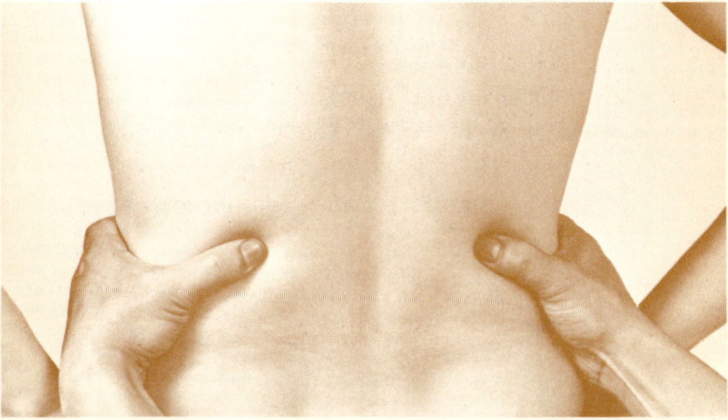

20 ABDOMINAL PAINS

1. NA of armpit.
2. NING around navel.
3. TUI A of waist. See photo (below) at page 19.
4. NA of shoulder blade. See photo (above) at page 19.

IF NEEDED: General Massage from waist downward.

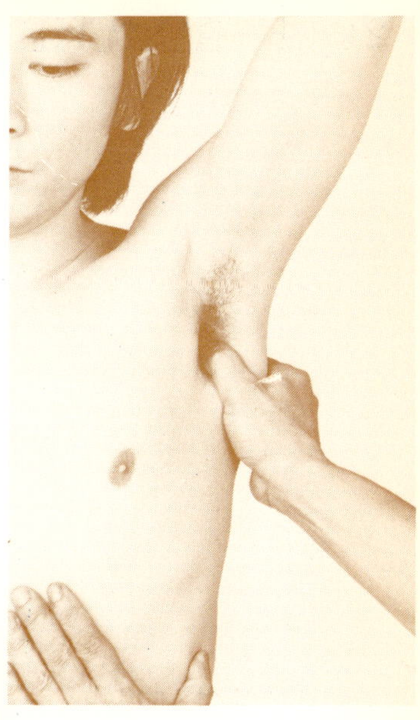

NA of armpit

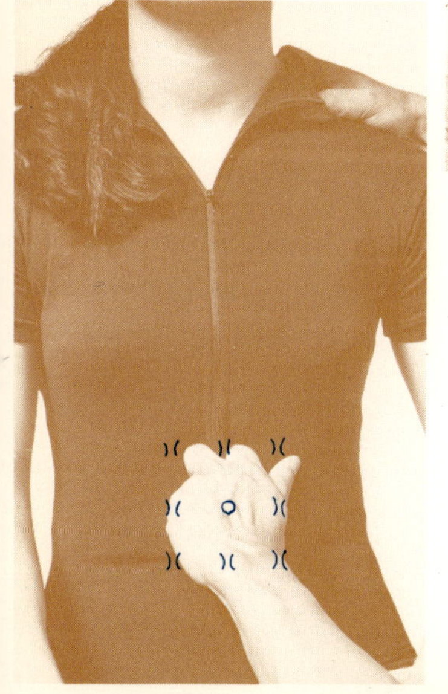

NING around navel

21 HEADACHE

Front of head :
1. General Massage TYPE ONE.
2. TUI A for forehead. (See page 5.)
3. NING between eyebrows. See photo (left.)

Side of head :
1. AN as shown at page 11.
2. TUI B or NING to sides of neck.

Mid-line of head :
TUI B or NING to mid-line of back of neck.
See photo (right.)

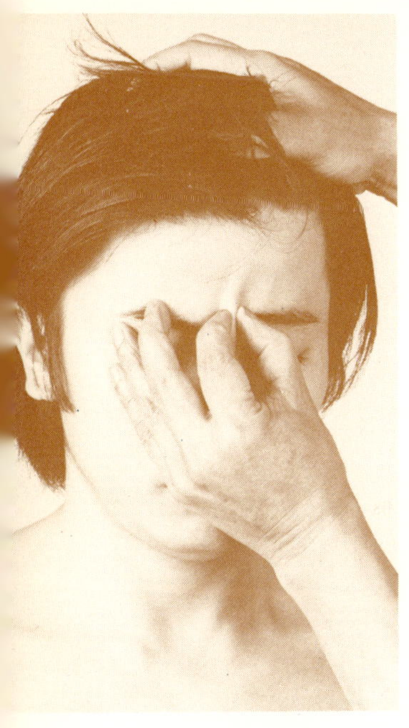

NING to back of neck

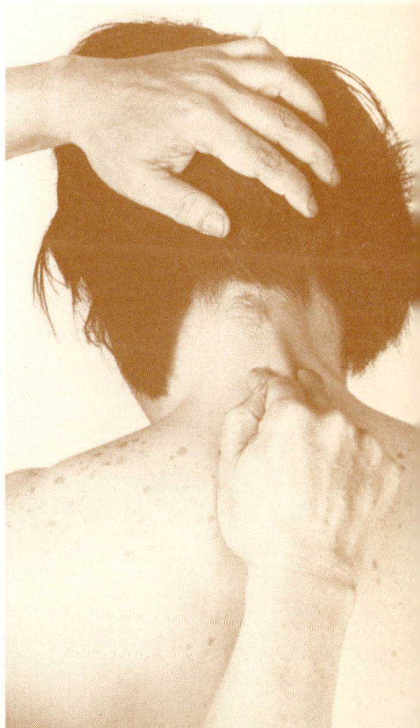

NING between eyebrows

22 ASTHMA

1. AN as shown in photo (left.)
2. General Massage TYPE TWO.

In ASTHMA attack :
1. TAO as shown at page 12.
2. TUI A of chest.
3. NING of throat and chest. See photo (right.)
4. AN to side of nose.

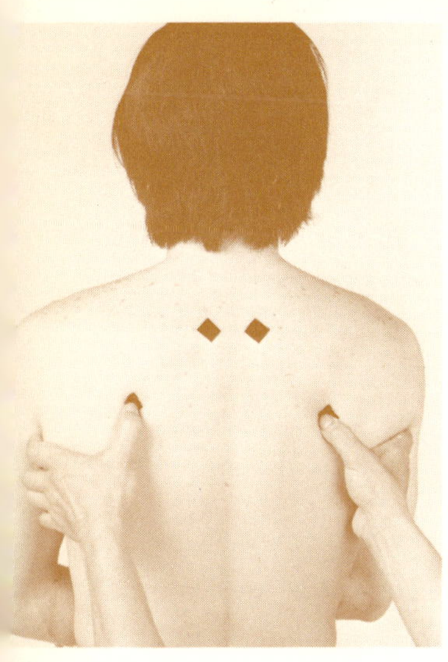

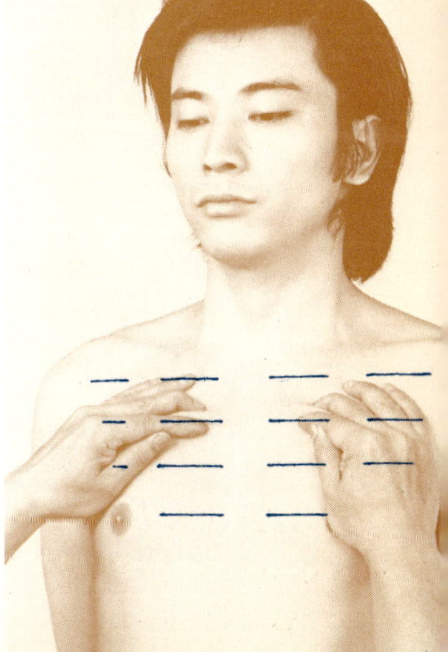

NING of chest

23 RHEUMATIC PAINS

1. General Massage.
2. TUI A of upper extremities (arms.) Modify and apply it to the pain location and intensity. See photo.
3. AN with warmed hands to all aspects of knee joint or any painful joint, and push from inside to outside.

TUI A of upper extremities

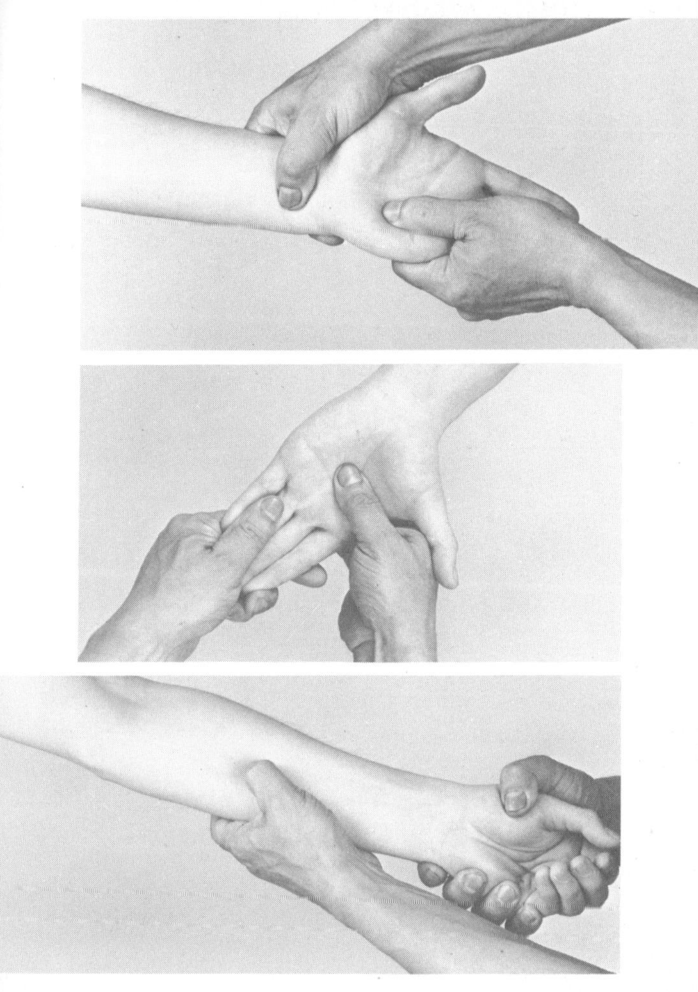

24 STIFF NECK

1. TUI B to upper shoulder.
2. General Massage TYPE TWO. Upper position only.
3. Light neck movements, 10 or 20 times, and suddenly turn head with quick movement.

BEFORE TREATING: Wrap the patient warmly and have him lie down and relax.

General Massage TYPE TWO

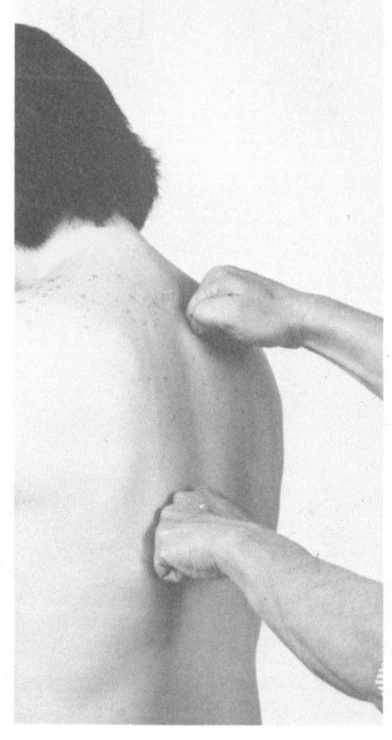

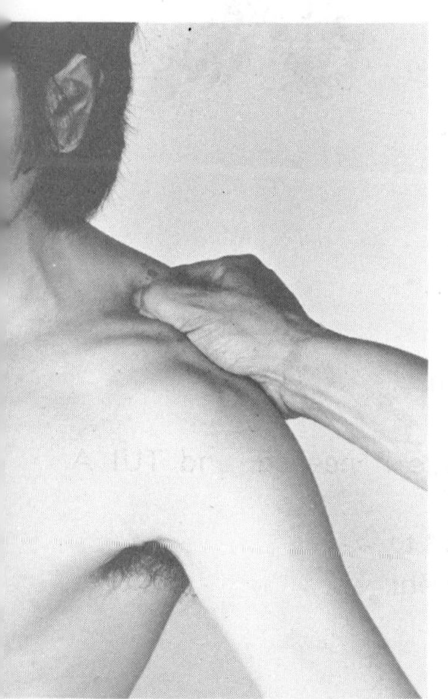

TUI B to upper shoulder

25 CHILDREN'S DISTURBED SLEEP

1. MA to abdomen.
2. NIE to back.
3. General Massage if needed, and TUI A of chest.
4. TAO of heel and toes.
5. TUI between eyebrows.

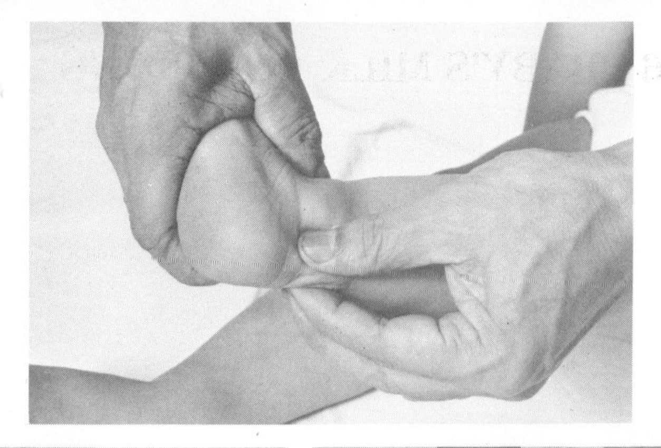

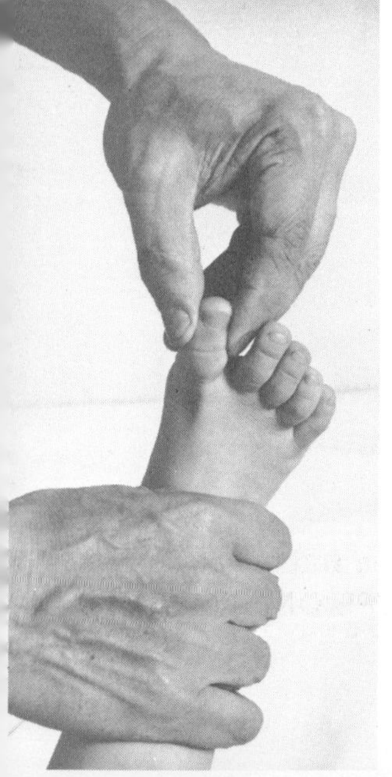
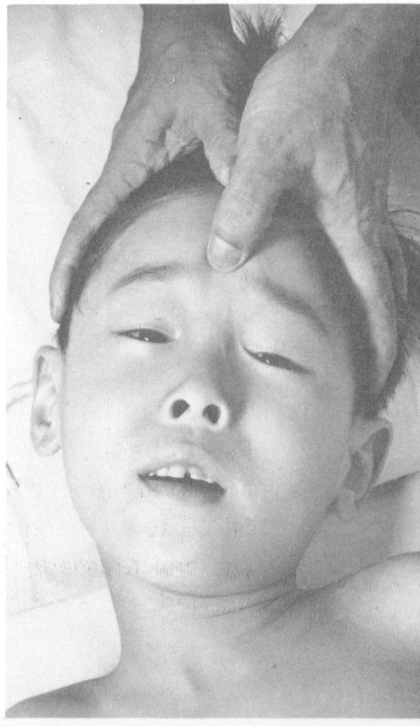

26 BABY'S MILK VOMITTING

1. TUI A of forehead.
2. PAI to back.
3. MA to abdomen.
4. NING to stomach area and throat.
5. General Massage TYPE ONE or TWO, if needed.

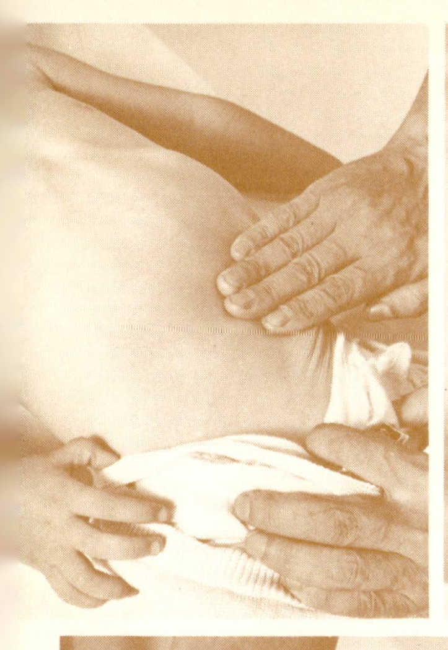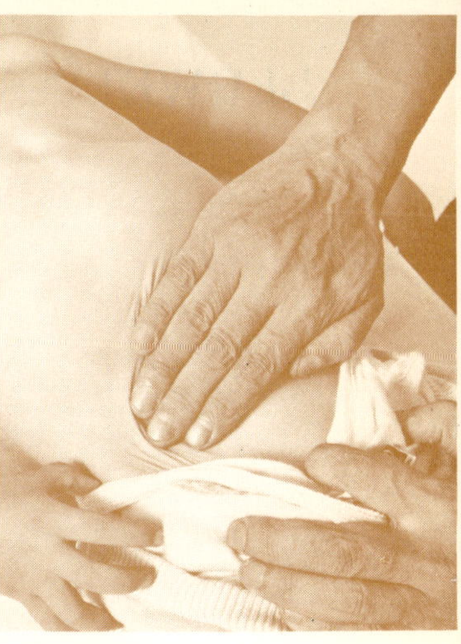

MA to abdomen

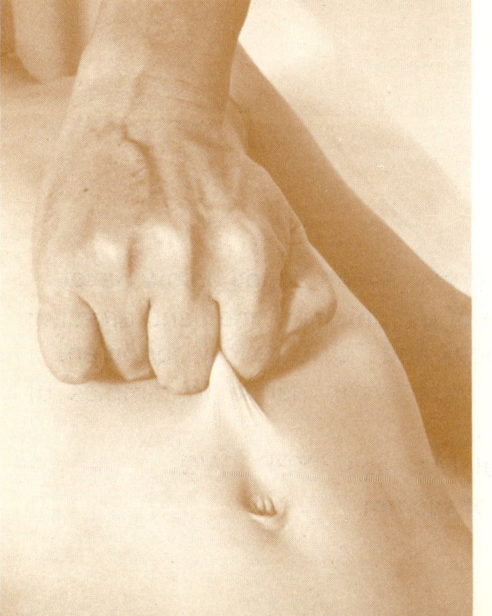

NING to stomach area

27 BEDWETTING

1. Pushing with warm hands below navel.
2. In case of girl children, one hand pressing on coccyx and TUI C of low abdomen.
3. TUI C with warm hands to dimples of sacrum.
4. General Massage TYPE TWO.
5. TUI C of sacrum.

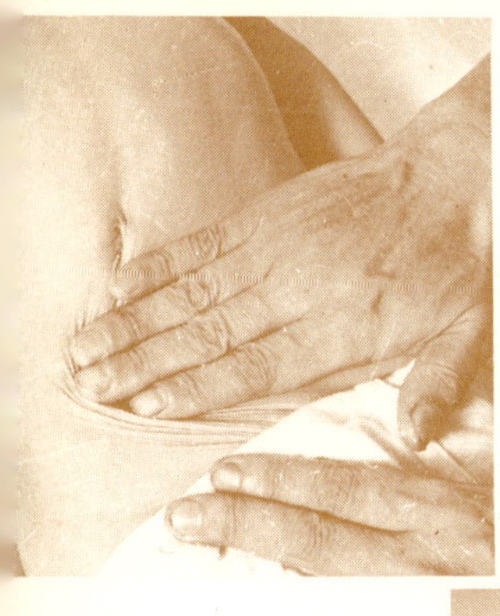

Pushing with warm hands

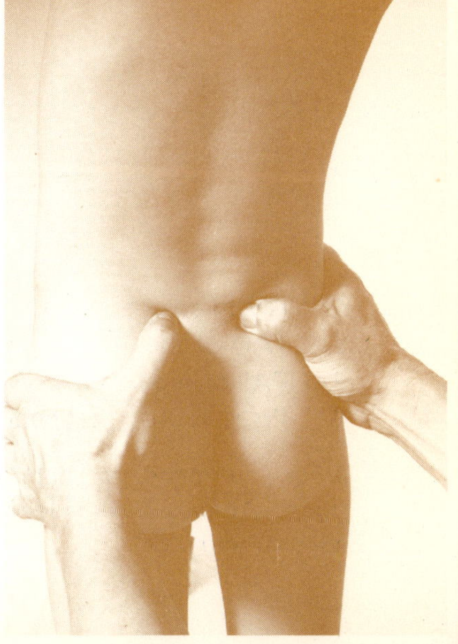

TUI C

to dimples of sacrum

28 NASAL BLEEDING

1. AN to side of nose.
2. TAO of toes.
3. PAI of forehead.
4. Press strongly on neck behind the ears.

Note: If menstrual period is disturbed and there is heavy nasal bleeding, add TUI C of sacrum and waist.

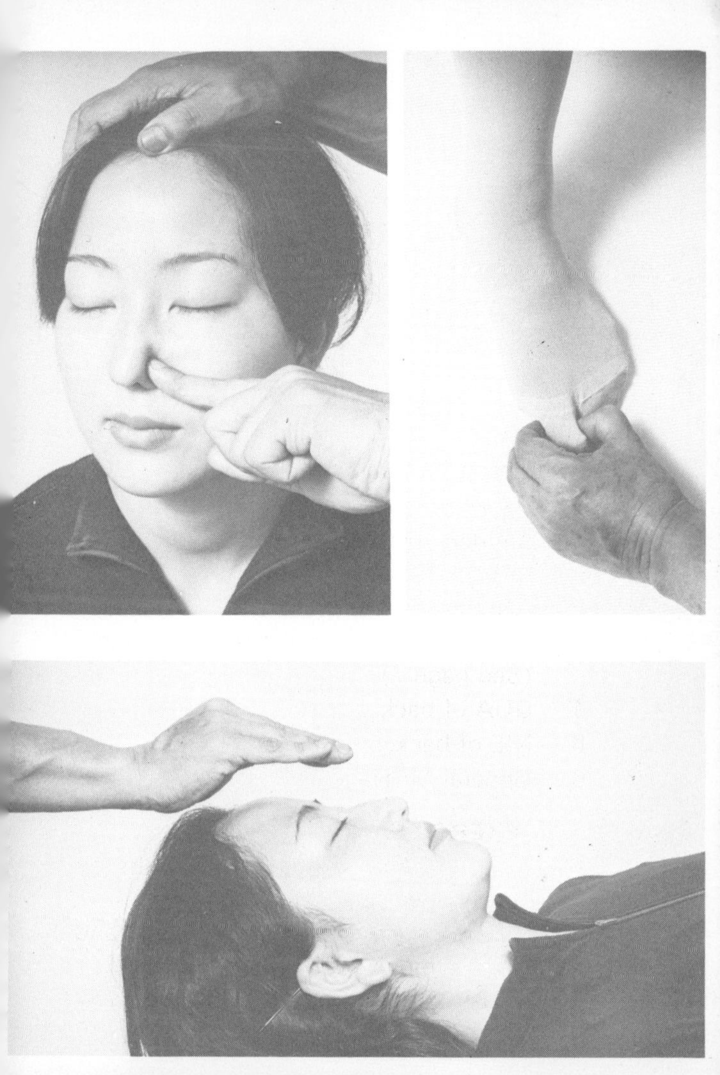

29 LUMBAGO

Patient prone or standing:

1. Have the knee bent 140° to 160°. Suddenly and unexpectedly strong PAI to back of knee.
2. AN to waist and knee.
3. GUA to side of waist and abdomen. (See page 7.)
4. GUA of back.
5. NIE of back.
6. General Massage TYPE TWO.

EXERCISE:

1. Stand, with body weight on heels.
2. Raise arms above head, and move body weight forward.
3. Rotate body 3 to 5 times.

EXERCISE
1
2
3
4

30 THROAT PAINS

1. NING or GUA to back of neck and down the spine.
2. NING to chest and temples.
    If right side of throat is painful, treat left and vice versa.
    If swallowing is difficult, the treatment is as shown in photo, pressing the patient's back against the operator's chest, and rubbing the clavicle with three fingers from the center outwards.

Note: Try to swallow some fluids, following this treatment. If necessary, repeat.

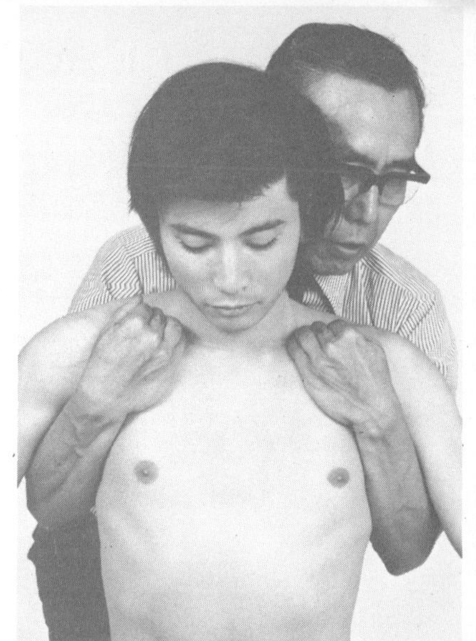

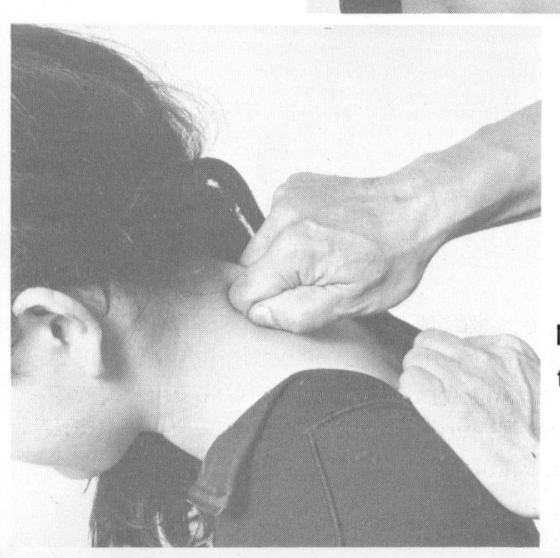

NING
to back of neck

31 ABOUT THE AUTHOR

The author, **Dr. Yoshio Manaka**, was born in 1911. After graduation from Kyoto University, he studied surgery at Tokyo University. In 1957, he took the degree of M.D. at Kyoto University.

He visited America, Europe and Africa many times, and now, he is one of the best-known authorities on Massage as well as Acupuncture.

Among his many books, there are English and French editions of "Acupuncture."

This pocketable book is his latest work intended for beginners, done in collaboration with his close friend, **Dr. Ian A. Urquhart**, who works for Tokyo Metropolitan Fuchu Institute of Rehabilitation.